TOP TIPS:
SHARING BIBLE STORIES

Sue Brown, Andy Gray, Gill Marchant

Copyright © Scripture Union 2008
First published 2008, reprinted 2010
ISBN 978 184427 328 7

Scripture Union England and Wales
207-209 Queensway, Bletchley, Milton
Keynes, MK2 2EB, England
Email: info@scriptureunion.org.uk
Website: www.scriptureunion.org.uk

Scripture Union Australia, Locked Bag
2, Central Coast Business Centre,
NSW 2252
Website: www.scriptureunion.org.au

Scripture Union USA
PO Box 987, Valley Forge, PA 19482
Website: www.scriptureunion.org

Scripture quotations are taken from
the HOLY BIBLE, NEW INTERNATIONAL
VERSION, (NIV), © 1973, 1978, 1984
by International Bible Society. Used by
permission of Hodder & Stoughton, a
division of Hodder Headline Ltd. All
rights reserved.

The right of Sue Brown, Andy Gray
and Gill Marchant to be identified as
authors of this work has been
asserted by them in accordance with
the Copyright, Designs and Patents
Act 1988.

British Library Cataloguing-in-
Publication Data: a catalogue record
of this book is available from the
British Library.

Printed and bound in Singapore by
Tien Wah Press Ltd

Logo, cover design, internal design:
www.splash-design.co.uk

Internal illustrations: Colin Smithson

Typesetting: Richard Jefferson,
Author and Publisher Services

Scripture Union is an
international Christian charity working
with churches in more than 130
countries, providing resources to bring
the good news about Jesus Christ to
children, young people and families
and to encourage them to develop
spiritually through the Bible and
prayer.

As well as our network of volunteers,
staff and associates who run holidays,
church-based events and school
Christian groups, we produce a wide
range of publications and support
those who use our resources through
training programmes.

Children matter facilitates cooperation
between all Christians who work with
children. For more details see
www.childrenmatter.net

CONTENTS

INTRODUCTION

Everyone has their own unique stories to tell, sometimes going back generations. Children can tell their own personal story but it will almost always be against the background of their own family or maybe their community or school. Stories are a part of our lives. It is therefore not surprising that we are fascinated by them.

We don't have to be a child to be captivated by a story being well told. Our whole lives are surrounded by stories – telling someone about our day, hearing news stories, watching soap operas or films. This book, however, is going to focus on how to share stories and specifically Bible stories, with children. Much of what it covers can be employed in sharing stories with young people and adults too.

Think about...

Can you remember the first story you were told? Where were you, who told it and how was it told? Make a list of everything that made this story memorable. Keep this list with you as you read this book and reflect on what it tells you.

Why tell stories?

Lots of research has been done on stories and how they help us make sense of the world. It is generally agreed that adults, young people and children alike, need stories to help unravel everyday experiences. Each new story joins the bank of stories, to draw on when we need to understand life.

Christians also believe that Bible stories are not just any stories but are special because they are the stories of God. By remembering and telling them, God becomes 'active in the storytelling event'. In other words, he does not remain just the God who appears in the story but through his activity as God, the Spirit, he creatively works in the present, as the storyteller and listeners encounter the story. If God is at work in this encounter, we can expect to be changed whether we are *listening* to the story or *telling* it.

In reality…
Sometimes while I am telling a story, God reveals something new to me that I had not previously thought of in my preparation. Often this new revelation challenges me about something in my own life. That's the privilege of being a storyteller.

One of the biggest challenges in sharing Bible stories with children is how we understand the word 'story'. A story can have any one of many meanings:

- Today's society tends to link story with fiction, stories which are not necessarily true. Children may therefore want to know if the Bible story we are telling is true. For this reason some use the word 'narrative' instead of 'story'.
- Telling stories or telling tales means telling lies or exaggerating or reporting someone's misbehaviour. This is a negative understanding of the word 'story', very much part of a child's experience!
- An account of a real life incident which may be part of someone's own experience – my story, our story, his story.
- A tale or story can be made up but is knowingly used to explain an event or idea. It may be helpful to explain if the Bible story we are telling is a fictional tale told to make a point like the parables, or an account of an actual event. We need to share if we are part of the story, as well as indicate what this story means to us personally.

WHAT THE BIBLE SAYS ABOUT STORYTELLING

Bible stories and the Bible story.

The Bible is full of stories so where should we begin? It is important to remember that every individual Bible story fits into the greater overarching narrative of the Bible. God's big story is about his relationship with the world he created: a story of creation, rebellion, redemption and restoration. The hero is God himself.

Some people in their children's work choose to travel through this big story from beginning to end, telling the individual stories in chronological order from Genesis and ending with Revelation. Others choose to explore themes or biblical characters and weave this larger story into the individual stories being shared.

The Bible speaks of sharing the stories of God with children, both explicitly and implicitly. Exodus 12:26 and Joshua 4:6 refer to occasions when the Israelites are charged with explaining to their children why they are doing a particular act or returning to a particular place. 'And when your children ask... then tell them...' In Psalm 78, the psalmist proclaims that he is not going to hide these stories but tell them to the coming generation. This is expanded in Joel 1:3 when God's people are told to pass the news on, not just to the next generation but to generations to come. 'Tell it to your children, and let your children tell it to their children, and their children to the next generation.' In the New Testament Jesus recognises that some stories will be told time and time again. In Matthew 26, a woman pours an alabaster jar of perfume over Jesus' head, and Jesus declares in verse 13 that 'wherever this gospel is preached throughout the world, what she has done will also be told, in memory of her.'

There are many references in the Old Testament to God being the God of history, the God of his people's story. In Exodus 3, Moses encounters God at the burning bush and God tells him, ' "I am the

God of your father, the God of Abraham, the God of Isaac, and the God of Jacob." ' As Moses stood there he must have been remembering all those stories he had heard about the God of his ancestors. In the light of this, he hears the commission to return to Egypt to lead the Israelites to the Promised Land.

As well as stories of people and their encounter with God, the Bible records stories which are told to explain a particular truth. For example, in 2 Samuel 12, the Old Testament prophet, Nathan, tells King David such a story. David is caught up in the parable of a rich man who took his neighbour's only lamb before realising this is a challenge to his own behaviour.

Think about...

If you have been a Christian a long time think about the Bible stories passed on to you. Who told them to you? Who, in the next generation, have you told? If you are a new Christian you may be asking, 'What do these stories mean to me?' Pray that as you seek to understand them and then explain them to others, you will all learn to love God more.

Jesus the storyteller

Jesus uses stories to teach his disciples, the people around him as well as the religious leaders of the day. His most famous stories are the parables but these were not the only stories he used to interact with his audience. He used Old Testament stories. For example, when challenged by the Pharisees in Mark 2 about picking corn to eat on the Sabbath, Jesus justifies his actions by drawing on the story when David ate the sacred bread that only priests should eat. In Luke 4, Jesus refers to the stories of Elijah being sent to a widow in Zarephath, and Elisha being sent to Naaman the Syrian, to make the point that no prophet is accepted in his home town. He also draws on contemporary events to highlight key points. Many people believe the householder in Luke 12, who had been burgled, was someone everyone present would have known.

As a storyteller, Jesus used images that were familiar to the listeners and drew on experiences that they understood. Through such familiar images and experiences he taught profound truths that were often complex and misunderstood. Even his followers needed to have them explained. Luke 18:34, 'they did not know what [Jesus] was talking about.' Jesus was challenging their preconceptions by allowing the story to speak for itself. He sometimes explained his parables to his followers but rarely to his wider audience.

Think about…
Are you tempted to explain the meaning of the stories you tell? Why not follow the example of Jesus and let the story speak for itself.

Of course, we also need to ensure that, as we retell all these stories of the people of the Bible and stories told by Bible characters, they connect with the lives and experiences of those listening to us now. We may need to explain elements that are no longer familiar to our listeners.

Make sure the children know that the story comes from the Bible. You may want to pinpoint where in the Bible they can find it. For more inspiration and ideas read *Top Tips on Exploring the Bible with children* and *Top Tips on Discovering the Bible with young people* (SU) 2008.

In reality...
I was telling the story of Ruth and Naomi to a group of children in an inner city school. Naomi's experience of leaving her home because of a famine, to live in another country was familiar to many there who had themselves moved from their wider family. Such personal experiences heightened their understanding of this story.

2 PRINCIPLES OF STORYTELLING

Choosing a Bible story

So many good stories to choose from, so how do you decide which to tell? Are all Bible stories suitable for children or do you need to be selective? For example, the story of Amnon and his incestuous relationship with his half-sister, Tamar (2 Samuel 13) would not be suitable for most children but with supportive parents present you might want to use it as a means of exploring abusive family relationships. With young people you may be more able to use this story. So the context and nature of the audience in the storytelling will affect your choice, as will the issue you want to highlight.

Scripture Union conducted a survey to discover the top ten Bible stories that most needed to be passed onto the next generation. The results in order of priority were as follows:

> Jesus' birth, Jesus' death and resurrection, creation and Adam and Eve, the good Samaritan, the ten commandments, the prodigal son, Noah's ark, David and Goliath, Daniel and the lions' den and feeding the 5000.

Any surprises? These have now been retold as the *Must Know Stories*, available for adults, 8–11s and 5–7s. For more details see page 32.

All Bible stories were written with the eyes of faith. They were designed not just to tell an account of what happened but also to explain it as part of God's story. For example, the stories of the individual kings in Kings and Chronicles were not a complete account of everything they did, but were chosen carefully to explain how God was at work in Israel.

New Testament writers knew their Scriptures (our Old Testament) and wrote in the light of those stories, often making references to them either obviously or subtly. The church right up to the present day reads and understands the Old Testament in the light of the incarnation, death and resurrection of Jesus, and stories told in the New Testament. This means that, for example, Christians have a clear interpretation of the stories about Moses and Abraham. A Jew or Muslim, for whom these are also important characters, might interpret such stories differently. This is very important to remember if we are telling stories in school during assemblies or in RE lessons.

Given freedom to choose a story for a school or church group, ask yourself the following questions. The answers will influence which stories you choose and how you tell them.

- Who is the audience?
- How old are they?
- Where are you telling the story?
- How long have you got?
- Do you know the children well, slightly or not at all?
- Have you told them stories before?
- Do they come from a Christian background and/or do they hear lots of Bible stories?
- Have you been given a theme to follow?

Think about...
Answer the questions opposite thinking about a group of children you know in church. What things should you consider when sharing a story with this group? Then think of some children in a different setting, such as a school or club. How might you share a story with them? Compare the two groups and what you will do with them.

Choosing a focus

We need to decide which elements to highlight in any story. Read the story carefully, if possible in more than one translation. Jot down all the things that can be drawn out of this story, trying to identify which are the most important to the writer. Choose which ones to focus on. The answers to the questions on page 11 may help to choose the focus. To explore this further, the Stapleford Centre has a very helpful booklet called *Concept cracking* which can be downloaded from the website www.e-stapleford.co.uk

In reality...
When telling the story of Ruth and Naomi in schools with pupils whose families were born overseas, I focused on God being with us even though we may be apart from the security of family and familiar culture. This influenced how the story was introduced and which points I emphasised.

Remembering the audience

A storytelling activity contains several encounters:
- the storyteller encounters the audience and vice versa
- everyone may encounter God
- the listeners encounter each other

When we tell a story we bring our understanding to the story which will become clear in the telling. Our audience also brings their previous understanding to the story. If their view of God, the world and themselves is different from ours, they may take away from the story a different message than the one we were expecting them to. This could alarm us but we need to realise that this is not a two-way but a three-way encounter: the storyteller, the listener and God. We can trust God to use the story. Someone once said of Bible stories that they go home to roost, often settling beyond consciousness, working their influence from below. How exciting is that?

Of course this is no excuse not to prepare thoroughly. We need to work hard to make as many connections as we can with the world of children listening to us.

> **In reality…**
> A school group of 46 11-year-old children were asked what they had learnt from the story of Noah. There were a variety of responses: 16 were challenged to take care of the world, 19 to consider their behaviour, 4 to consider God and 6 empathised with the plight of the animals, or saw Noah as a role model. Only one pupil was not challenged at all.

Being a good storyteller

We can read Bible stories and there are some very good Bible storybooks available for all ages. Story reading involves a book being open for us, as the reader, to convey word for word the intent and emotion of the writer. Reading well, using a variety of pace, accent, volume and personal enthusiasm is a skill in itself. A picture book adds an additional prop to the storytelling.

Storytelling without reading allows us to add our own understanding, emotions and words. It gives freedom to emphasise parts relevant to a particular audience and use words and concepts that they can understand. We are able to share part of ourselves in the telling of the story – how it affected us when we first heard it, what the story means to us. We can tell it in such a way that matches the learning styles of our listeners – do they prefer thinking, experiencing and sharing, or doing something practical? All these can be introduced into a story session.

The art of good storytelling is to tell it from memory. Glancing down at the text will actually detract from the whole telling and listening experience. Remember every story has:

- a beginning, to set out the main characters, the period of history it comes from, the context of the story, and tensions that there may be between characters or within just one character.
- a middle, which describes the way characters develop or learn something about themselves or each other. It identifies further conflicts and sets us up for ...
- an end, where there is a resolution of conflicts which may be happy or sad, or leave us with more questions.
- a question or challenge such as, 'What about you?'

In reality...

When learning a new story I will sometimes write it out, sometimes draw quick pictures like a storyboard and, sometimes tell it over and over to myself until I find the right words... often in the shower!

PRACTICAL IDEAS

How much of the story can be told?

Make sure that the point being made is actually in the Bible text. It can be very tempting to draw points from other parts of the Bible that, if we are honest, are not really emphasised in the text we are using. For example, the point of the story of Jesus' encounter with Zacchaeus in Luke 19 is not that he loves small people and therefore loves children. That may be true but Luke implies that in the previous chapter.

A Bible story should not be used as a coat hanger from which we hang whatever 'lesson' we want to impart. The Bible does not exist to reinforce our own ideas!

We need to ensure that we are emphasising and telling the whole story as painted in the Bible and not leave out parts that we may feel less comfortable with. A speaker asked a group of children's workers if they had told the story of the boy Samuel hearing from God (1 Samuel 3:1–11). Almost every hand went up. The speaker then asked how many had also told what God said to Samuel once he finally listened to him (1 Samuel 3:12–18). Not one hand remained up.

Preparation

Read the Bible passage
Read the story in several different versions and read a couple of commentaries on the passage if you can. You can access many versions of the Bible and commentaries through the Internet but ask your church leader for advice on good commentaries, Bible dictionaries and atlases – see page 32 for suggestions. If you are serious about helping children and young people engage with the Bible you will probably be thinking about getting your own reference material.

Looking at different versions helps to see different emphases in the way a story is phrased. Commentaries help to explain the background and interpret the story. This not only sparks the imagination but helps you remain true to the original context of the story. For example, anyone telling the story of Nehemiah rebuilding the walls of Jerusalem needs to know the historical and geographical background of the situation.

Look at the story from different points of view
You can look at a story from the perspective of various characters in a story. If it is a well known story, consider telling it from a different perspective. For example, the story of Jesus' trial could be told from the perspective of Pontius Pilate.

Consider whether to tell the story in the first or third person

Think about…
Choose a minor character in a Bible story and think about how they would view the events. How could you tell this story from this person's perspective?

To assume you are the character makes it more personal but can be forced. If you are telling the story in character, decide how to communicate this character to your audience – eg using a different pitch of voice, an accent, a costume, a prop or a distinct mannerism. Page 24 gives more advice on using the voice.

Write out the story
It can help to write out your story script in advance. This can clarify it in your own mind so you know exactly what you want to say. You can then make any necessary adjustments and be really sure you are

familiar with it. Try to learn the story you are telling so as to avoid simply reading it. If you can't memorise the story, jot down just the key moments as a prompt.

Starting the story

Will you jump straight into it? Will you start in a particular character? Will you introduce it as a story from the Bible? Will you explain its meaning before you begin? Begin in a way that captures the attention of the audience. If it is a Bible story, it is essential not to begin with 'once upon a time' which is a phrase associated with fairy stories. Needless to say, Bible stories come from a different culture and era so some background information may be essential.

Ending the story

Decide on your closing sentence and try to stick to it. Try to end with the audience wanting more.

There are different opinions about whether to explain the meaning of a story or leave it for the listener to work it out. Jesus rarely added a moral or explanatory note (with the exception of the parable of the farmer and the seed in Mark 4). But his audience often got the point (for example, the good Samaritan in Luke 10). A memorable story, told well, will live in the minds of the hearer for hours if not days, giving them time to reflect on it and even retell it to others. The Holy Spirit is active in the memory of every hearer, making it possible for anyone to hear from God. If, however, you suspect the listeners might misunderstand or take unhelpful meanings from the story, it is probably worth clarifying what you feel are the main points.

Usually the main point is put at the end, but some children lose concentration once they think the story has finished and will miss your point! Try putting the main point in the middle, crafting it into the telling in the form of a question. It could be part of setting the scene, or giving the opportunity to look out for a particular character, or a change of attitude or behaviour. If you set the scene in this way, pick up on the question at the end and see who spotted the answer.

In reality…
At the start, I asked the children to decide who the person of courage was in the story of David meeting with Abigail and her husband, Nabal (1 Samuel 25). After sharing the story I asked the question again and let the children explain why Abigail was the real person of courage.

Practise telling the story to yourself or a friend.
If possible, stand in front of a mirror, or ask a friend, to observe your facial expressions and body movements. It may be embarrassing, but all practise has value. It will point out oddities and helps build confidence.

Think how to help children understand the story
Bible stories come from other cultures and centuries, and listeners may require help to relate to the events of the story. Simple questions help children interact

In reality…
When telling any Biblical story that involves a journey, I remind children that this was before the time of cars, trains or aeroplanes. People walked or rode on a donkey to get around.

with emotions. For example, Naaman was probably very surprised when he was healed in the way that he was. Asking listeners if they have ever had an unexpected surprise birthday party, or a visit from someone special, will help them associate their own feelings with what Naaman might have experienced. To share your own emotional responses to stories also enables the listeners to make connections.

Tools for storytelling

There are broadly three ways in which people may take in information: visually (by what they see); aurally (by what they hear); kinaesthetically (by active engagement). These are not tightly applied to any one person, but worth considering in our storytelling, allowing for listening, looking and engagement. For example, words or pictures evoke visual images and memories, tone and use of voice appeal to an aural response while using actions to keywords may later remind listeners of the story. We don't have to include all of these activities every time, only as appropriate.

Think about...
How might your storytelling be affected if you used these three learning styles? Discuss this with others you know who work with children and young people.

Pictures or illustrations
Pictures are an excellent and well-tried way to keep drawing people back into a story. Use pictures in colour or bold black and white, in as high a quality as possible, making them big enough to be seen at the back of the group.

Props and visual aids

Basically anything can be used to maintain attention and help the memory. So for example, before telling a story lay out various objects on a table that relate in some way to the story. Alternatively, conceal objects in a story bag or container. The objects are shown or revealed at the right moment.

Puppets

Puppets connect with people in a unique way and can often reach some of the most unreachable of children. Puppets can be used to tell or act out stories, as an introduction to a theme or to discuss the meaning of a story. Puppetry training is available across the country and, if you are considering using puppets, it is worth booking onto a course to help build up your skills. For more details visit http://www.onewayuk.com

Before choosing a puppet, think about what characteristics the puppet will have and choose one whose appearance suits the character. Practise using your puppet in front of a mirror. This will help you see the puppet as others see it, in order to develop appropriate movements and mannerisms.

- If the puppet is 'speaking' make sure you, the storyteller, look at the puppet and that the puppet makes 'eye contact' with the audience. Research has shown that children relate better to puppets that 'speak' than to puppets that whisper in someone's ear.

- When the puppet 'speaks', its lips need to move for roughly the correct amount of syllables it is speaking. For example, if a puppet is 'saying' a long sentence but only opens its mouth once, children see something is wrong and the relationship between them and the puppet will be damaged.

- The puppet does not 'freeze' when it isn't speaking. It needs to keep looking around or moving even when something else is happening.

Shadow puppets are an effective and ancient medium for telling stories. All you need are puppets, a screen and a light. Pre-record the tale and use the shadow puppets to act it out. It is a refreshing alternative to modern technology. For more information see artsedge.kennedy-center.org/shadowpuppets/artsedge.html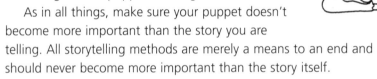

As in all things, make sure your puppet doesn't become more important than the story you are telling. All storytelling methods are merely a means to an end and should never become more important than the story itself.

Use repetition

Repetition can be useful in maintaining attention – particularly with younger children. Repeated key phrases or actions can be built into the story. Not only do these help keep attention but can be used to re-emphasise the main point. A catchphrase, repeated more than once, invites the listeners to join in.

The number three

Many European folk stories use groups of threes as a central feature of a story – for example, *Goldilocks and the Three Bears or The Three Little Pigs*. Good stories often have three main characters, three wishes or three answers to a problem. Storyteller, Chris King, suggests that the use of threes in a story allows for a balance of options, characters or diversity. It works! So consider using three characters, or giving three possible answers to a question, or three responses spoken by the characters. Try using different numbers of things and see if there is any difference in your audience's response. For more details see www.creativekeys.net/StorytellingPower/article1004.html

Presentation and delivery

Resources and technology

Your storytelling session can be enhanced with the use of technology. You could use music to set the scene as you tell a story, or a PowerPoint presentation of images relevant to the action you are describing. You could create the story using cartoon pictures and tell the story as they appear on the screen.

If you do want to use these things, make sure all resources and props are fully prepared, easily accessible, working properly, safe to use and in the right order. This certainly applies to technological and electrical equipment which has a nasty habit of going wrong. Use your own equipment if at all possible since you know how it works! Whatever happens you don't want the equipment to interfere with the process of storytelling. If you are relying on equipment supplied by others, arrive a few minutes before the start of a session or event, to explore how it works or to explain to the operator what you need. If there are changes to be made, agree a signal to indicate the change rather than break the rhythm of the story.

Technology, however brilliant, does not have to be used all the time. Sometimes the simplest of props or no props are more effective. See the section on Godly Play on page 28 for a good example of this approach.

Using the body

Stand still or move around? A good reason to use movement is to indicate different locations in the story. Two characters could stand in different places. But too much moving around can be confusing and can communicate nervousness or unease on the part of the storyteller.

Sit down or stand up? The size of the audience, the shape of the room and the expectation to use visual aids or not, will all affect this. It helps to be as close as possible to maintain eye contact, so being on a comfortable level with the children helps. Ultimately it is what feels comfortable for the storyteller.

Eye contact? One of the key skills of a storyteller is the ability to make eye contact with the audience. Frequent eye contact also helps to maintain discipline and concentration. The experienced storyteller uses this interaction with the audience to give clues on how to develop the story. Using a screen or visual aid can break eye contact, although shy or anxious children may prefer to fix their gaze upon a puppet or screen rather than a person, the storyteller.

Facial expressions? If you are using eye contact in your storytelling you need to be aware of your facial expressions. The face communicates lots of information. An audience is able to read these non-verbal signs. Think about how you can use them in your story and practise so that they flow easily as you tell the story.

Arm movements and body language? Think about what actions you want to include in your story and practise telling the story using these actions. Ask someone to watch the first time you tell the story and discuss whether the actions help the listener receive the story you are telling. You may have small movements or habits

Think about...
Consider your own body language next time you tell a story. How much do you move? What does your body language communicate to the listeners? Borrow a book on body language from the library to help you communicate your stories.

that you are unaware of which may detract from your storytelling. Try to avoid 'closed' body language that might damage your relationship with the audience. For example, avoid standing with your arms folded whilst you tell a story.

Using the voice

Pace: Pace or speed, used effectively, helps the listener understand what is important in the story and what is not so important. Pace is communicated by the speed of the words spoken, the actual words used (short and sharp or lengthy phrases) or the type of language. For example, increase the pace by using brief descriptions, and slow down the pace by using detailed descriptions and dialogue. Slowing the pace down is most effective where you want the listener to reflect on a point in the story, perhaps where you want them to put themselves in the place of the character, or when it follows a particularly fast piece of storytelling. To speed up the storytelling will show the urgency that the characters are experiencing or your desire to move on to the next important event.

Pitch: For lighter, fun moments, or for stressful moments use a higher pitch. That doesn't mean squeaking! When we get excited or when something upsets us, our bodies get tense, with the result that our vocal chords grow tense. This results in the pitch of our voice rising. When we are relaxed the voice is natural and soft. When we are cross

Think about...

Listen to someone telling a story and notice how they use their voice to create the mood of the story. Note down when and how they speed up or slow down and what effect it has.

we breathe in more air. Our windpipe expands to accommodate this, which means our vocal chords become more open, so the voice pitch drops below our natural speaking voice, sometimes sounding rougher. In storytelling we can emulate these effects to help listeners recognise the different emotions or situations we are conveying.

Silence: Silence creates a mood. Used in the right place we might literally 'hear a pin drop'. Maybe it is the moment when a character realises something for the first time, or perhaps a great moment of resolution has happened after internal or external conflict. Silence can bring about anticipation or leave space for the listener to ask themselves, "What will happen next? What would I do in that situation?"

Accent and dialect: Character voices and accents need to be done well so keep to what you are confident with and gradually work on new styles. So, for example, experiment with a different accent for a non-major character rather than getting it wrong for the main character. Take care with using accents and character voices because they can result in unhelpful stereotypes and can cause offence.

Using the audience

Members of the audience can help to tell the story. They can act out the characters whilst the story is told. They don't have to speak. They can read out key phrases and hold up slogans or pictures. Be sensitive in choosing children to participate,  considering their personality, abilities and circumstances. Avoid embarrassing an adult or undermining the authority of a teacher by asking them to do something unsuitable. You may be able to ask all volunteers before the session if they are happy to take part, and you can outline for them what they will have to do. In a school setting this may not be possible.

Watch how your audience responds to certain words, phrases or parts of the story. It will help improve your storytelling skills, especially when you next tell this story. The story will sometimes tell itself as you interact with your audience and new and different things occur to you as you tell it. Don't be afraid of responding to the prompting of the Holy Spirit as you tell the story. But always be true to the story and always be mindful of the context.

If your audience is becoming bored or wriggly, as often happens with younger audiences, move quickly onto the next piece of action. If they are engrossed in the story you can afford to spend more time on description. You may need to lengthen or shorten the story in different contexts which will affect the amount of detail you include, and the pace.

Types of storytelling

There are many different ways of telling Bible stories.

Using the imagination

Whether we are reading stories or listening to them we use our imagination. In our mind's eye we are visualising the scene(s) set before us. Some Bible stories are written in such a way that the author has given us clues to help us visualise what is happening. Consider Mark's account of the feeding of the 5,000 (Mark 6) where they all 'sit down in groups on the green grass'. The account of David's life in 1 and 2 Samuel is full of rich language that carries the story and helps us imagine the scene.

Even if the Biblical account is brief we can still help listeners to use their imagination. For instance, taking the journey of Joseph and Mary from Nazareth to Bethlehem, think about the length and breadth of the road. Was it a level or a winding road, going through valleys or over hills? What might it have felt like to be in a country occupied by the Romans? How might a heavily pregnant woman have coped? Reference books help to add factual information to shape and feed the imagination. By using the imagination everyone can feel part of the story, not just take in the factual events of it.

> ### In reality...
>
> Once I forgot to share a vital piece of information at the beginning of a story. When I realised this, I didn't stop but appropriately inserted this piece of information in the narrative and carried on. No one noticed but I remembered for the next time I told the story.

Multi-sensory stories

We can help people connect with stories in new ways by involving all the senses in the telling. This approach works especially well with people who have heard the story many times before. It enables the storyteller to move the audience from being passive to being an active part of the process which encourages more people to engage.

Xpedition Force, the SU holiday club based on Matthew's account of the week leading up to the crucifixion, uses a different sense for each of the five sessions: hearing for the sounds of Jesus' ride into Jerusalem; smell for the perfume poured over Jesus' feet; taste for the last supper; touch for the betrayal and crucifixion; sight for the resurrection. This is a powerfully effective approach to communicating the story.

Scripture Union has produced a wide range of books, filled with ideas on how to use all the senses in different aspects of church life – including storytelling. For more details go to page 32 or visit the website www.scriptureunion.org.uk.

In reality…

In Yorkshire, a youth worker downloaded some sounds of waves and a storm. She played them to her group as she read out a narrative of the calming of the storm. Members closed their eyes to picture the scene. At various points she asked them to think about how they would think and feel in this situation. Many said they had connected with the story in a way they hadn't done before.

Godly play

Godly play storytelling was developed in the United States by Dr Jerome Berryman from a variation of the Montessori tradition of education. A key part to regular storytelling is the storyteller himself, but this is not the case in *Godly play* where the storyteller takes a back seat and does not make eye contact with the audience. The story and the listener become the focus. This is achieved by using simple figures such as wooden shapes, coloured materials and open-ended questions that encourage wondering and response. In this approach, the storyteller purposely does not tell the participants the meaning or point of the story. Instead the group are encouraged to reflect on the story and draw their own conclusions – the story speaks for itself. At the end of each *Godly play* session children are encouraged to retell and explore the story in their own way using a variety of multi-sensory activities. To find out more visit www.godlyplay.org.uk

Bringing a character to life

This is an excellent way of bringing stories to life, but requires a lot of time and effort to get it right. Tell the story in the first person as either a Biblical character or an imaginary character who may have been viewing the scene. You need to research and explore how the character would react, to ensure you understand their motivations and emotions. Writing out what you want to say as a monologue or script is probably essential. It is important to use the right tense when telling stories in this way. Ask someone to read what you have written and comment afterwards on how it went. Perhaps this form of storytelling is closer to acting than telling a story. It is all too easy to overact, and then the performance becomes more important than the story. It would be sad for the listeners to say what a wonderful actor you were but they couldn't remember what it was you said!

Open the book

This is a storytelling project for primary school children based on stories taken from the *Lion Storyteller Bible* by Bob Hartman and other storybooks produced especially for this project. The aim is to present Bible stories in school assemblies using a variety of storytelling techniques. The project created enough material to visit schools weekly for three years. It begins with 'the big picture' and tells stories about the whole Bible and then focuses on 'Jesus and the early church' and 'Heroes, Heroines and Children in the Bible' during the subsequent years.

All the material has been designed specifically for volunteers from local churches to be able to present the Bible in an accessible and enjoyable way to children in schools. It is a great means of encouraging new people to share stories with children. Training and support is available as well as all the material you may need. Visit www.glosdioc.org.uk/Departments/Parish%20Resources/Children/Chotb.html for more information.

Father, thank you that through the Bible you have shared with us the greatest story ever told.

Thank you for the honour of being able to pass this story on to others.

Help us to share Bible stories in ways that communicate your love to all who hear.

May the stories we tell bring great honour to your name.

Amen

TEN TOP TIPS

1. Be true to the Bible. Read the Bible story carefully and make sure your retelling is true to both this story and the wider story of the Bible.

2. Prepare thoroughly considering your audience and their needs. Plan how you are going to begin and end the story. Decide which elements of the story you are going to focus on and how you are going to tell it.

3. Make sure the children know that the story comes from the Bible.

4. Pray that the storytelling session will be an opportunity for God to work in the lives of everyone present.

5. Practise telling the story with any visual aids that you have chosen to use.

6. Check your equipment works before you begin and can be seen and heard by all the audience.

7. Tell the story, rather than read it. Don't be afraid to be creative or to tell it slightly differently with each telling.

8. Use your body, eyes and voice to help create the mood and relationship with the audience.

9. Aim to go on improving your skills as a storyteller.

10. Relax and enjoy the encounter.

RESOURCES

Resource books
Ian Birkinshaw, *Multi-sensory Parables*, SU, 2006
Doug Swanney, *Xpedition Force*, SU, 2003 (holiday club material)
Bob Hartman, *Anyone Can Tell a Story*, Lion Hudson, 2002
David and Pat Alexander, *The Lion Handbook to the Bible*, Lion Hudson, 2002

Bible storybooks
Bob Hartman, *The Lion Storyteller Bible*, Lion Hudson, 2001
Robert Harrison, *The Strong Tower*, SU, 2006
Alexander Brown, *The Red Book of Must Know Stories*, SU, 2008 (for 5 to 7s)
Alexander Brown, *The Green Book of Must Know Stories*, SU, 2008 (for 5 to 7s)
Heather Butler, *The 10 Must Know Stories*, SU, 2008 (for 8 to 11s)
Robert Harrison, *The Must Know Stories*, SU, 2008 (for adults)
Big Bible Story Book, SU, 2007 (for under 8s)
Rhona Davies, *The Barnabas Children's Bible*, BRF, 2007

Useful websites
www.childrenmatter.net
Puppets:
www.thepuppetstore.com
www.puppetsbypost.com
http://puppetgallery.com
artsedge.kennedy-center.org/shadowpuppets/artsedge.html
Other:
www.godlyplay.org.uk – for godly play
www.glosdioc.org.uk/Departments/Parish%20Resources/Children/chotb.html – for Open the Book
www.stapleford-centre.org – The Stapleford Centre